WITHDRAWN

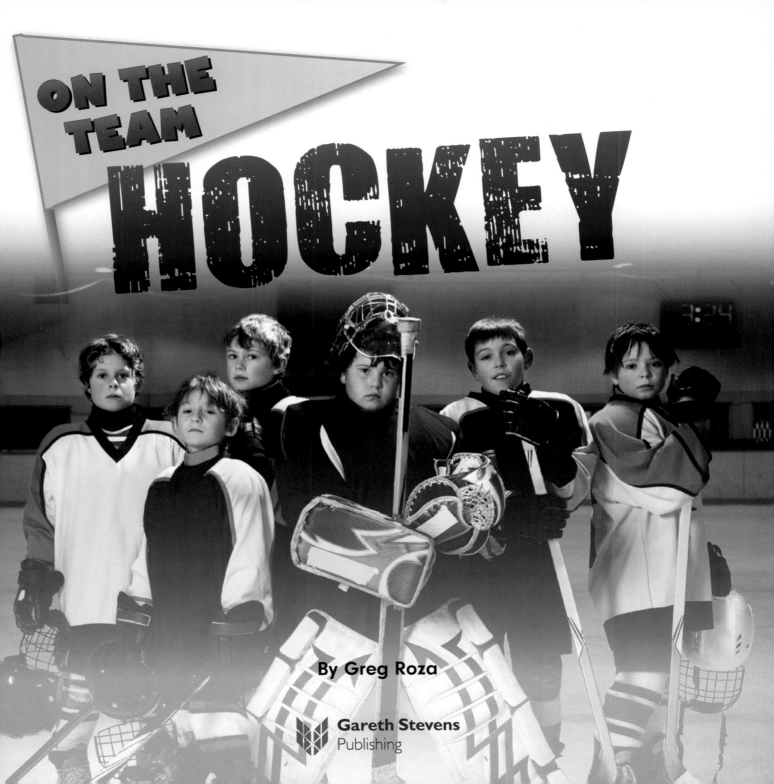

ON THE TEAM

HOCKEY

By Greg Roza

Gareth Stevens
Publishing

Please visit our website, www.garethstevens.com. For a free color catalog of all our high-quality books, call toll free 1-800-542-2595 or fax 1-877-542-2596.

Library of Congress Cataloging-in-Publication Data

Roza, Greg.
Hockey / Greg Roza.
    p. cm. — (On the team)
Includes index.
ISBN 978-1-4339-6450-3 (pbk.)
ISBN 978-1-4339-6451-0 (6-pack)
ISBN 978-1-4339-6448-0 (library binding)
1. Hockey—Juvenile literature. I. Title.
GV847.25.R698 2012
796.962—dc23
                                            2011027473

First Edition

Published in 2012 by
Gareth Stevens Publishing
111 East 14th Street, Suite 349
New York, NY 10003

Designer: Michael J. Flynn
Editor: Greg Roza

Photo credits: Cover, pp. 1, 13 iStockphoto.com; p. 5 (hockey players) Foto011/ Shutterstock.com; pp. 5 (puck), 14, 17, 21 Shutterstock.com; p. 6 Buyenlarge/ Archive Photos/Getty Images; p. 10 Grant Faint/The Image Bank/Getty Images; p. 18 Ryan McVay/Photodisc/Getty Images; p. 20 Rick Stewart/Getty Images.

Printed in the United States of America

CPSIA compliance information: Batch #CW12GS: For further information contact Gareth Stevens, New York, New York at 1-800-542-2595.

Contents

Words in the glossary appear in **bold** type the first time they are used in the text.

Pass, Shoot, Score!

Hockey is a team sport that's played on an ice surface called a rink. Hockey players wear ice skates. They use special sticks to pass a puck around the rink until they can shoot it into a goal for a point.

A hockey team has 20 players, but only six players are on the ice at one time. The action is fast, and the players on the ice get tired very quickly. Teammates work together to score points.

THE COACH'S CORNER

There are different kinds of hockey. Field hockey is played on grass. In roller hockey, players wear roller skates. This book is about ice hockey.

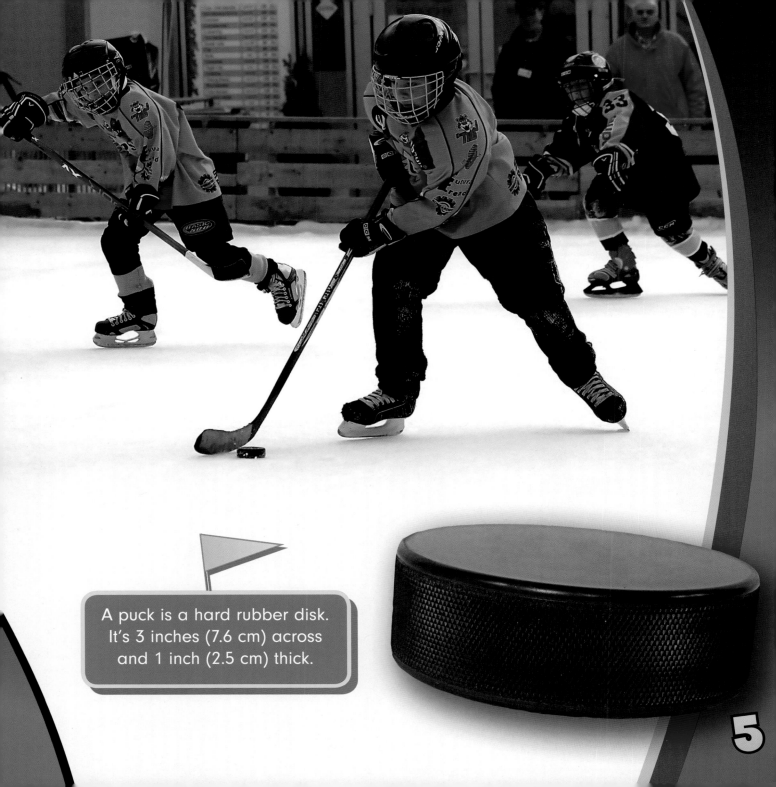

A puck is a hard rubber disk. It's 3 inches (7.6 cm) across and 1 inch (2.5 cm) thick.

This friendly hockey game took place in 1912 in New Bedford, Massachusetts.

6

Hockey History

Most historians believe hockey began in Canada. In the early 1800s, British soldiers in Canada played several ball-and-stick games, including a game similar to field hockey. Some began playing the game on ponds covered with ice. The first reported indoor hockey game happened in March 1875.

By the late 1800s, ice hockey had become a popular sport in Canada and the United States. Today, hockey is an Olympic sport, and **professional** hockey is played in countries around the world.

THE COACH'S CORNER

People still like to play ice hockey outside. It's sometimes called "pond hockey."

Face Off!

goal

An ice rink is a rectangular playing area with rounded corners. There's a goal at each end. Two blue lines split a rink into three different **zones**. The area closest to a team's own goal is the **defending** zone. The zone in the middle is the **neutral** zone. The area farthest from a team's goal is the attacking zone.

A rink has five circles—one in the center and two on either end. These are used for face-offs.

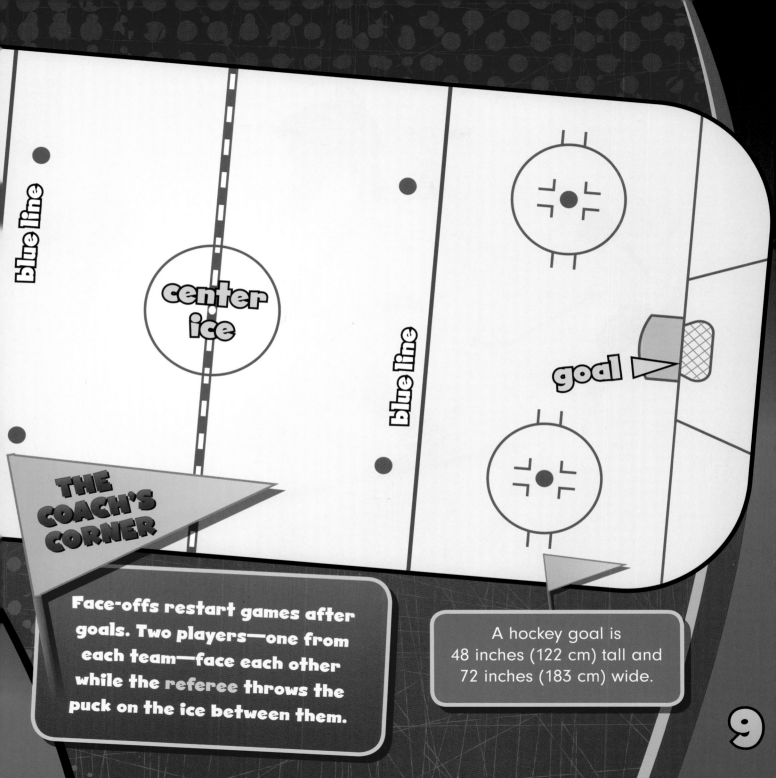

blue line

center ice

blue line

goal ▷

9

THE COACH'S CORNER

Face-offs restart games after goals. Two players—one from each team—face each other while the **referee** throws the puck on the ice between them.

A hockey goal is 48 inches (122 cm) tall and 72 inches (183 cm) wide.

This goalie makes a great save during an exciting game.

Get in the Game

A hockey game has three periods. Each period is 20 minutes long. The clock stops when someone gets hurt, after goals, and during **penalties**.

To score, players on a team use their sticks to shoot the puck into the other team's goal. That's called offense. Players also try to keep the other team from shooting the puck into their goal. That's called defense. During a fast-paced hockey game, teams change back and forth between offense and defense very quickly.

THE COACH'S CORNER

Passing the puck is an important part of hockey. A good pass can give a teammate a better chance to score a goal.

Playing Offense

On offense, players skate toward the other team's goal. They pass the puck back and forth, looking for a chance to shoot. They can take slap shots by raising their sticks and shooting the puck hard. They can take wrist shots by shooting the puck quickly without lifting their sticks.

Offensive players must be good skaters to get around the other team. They must have good stick-handling skills to keep the other team from stealing the puck from them.

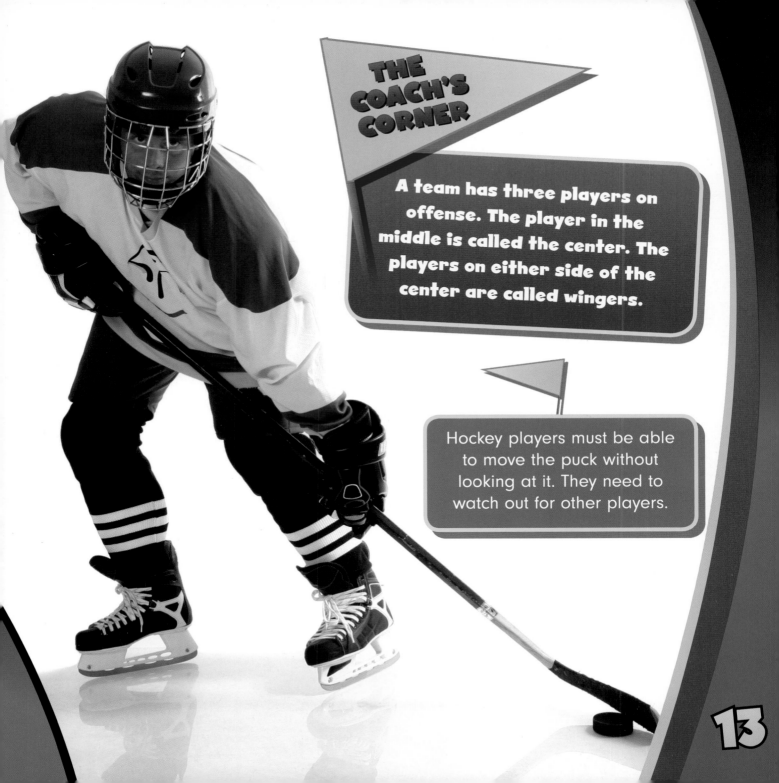

A team has three players on offense. The player in the middle is called the center. The players on either side of the center are called wingers.

Hockey players must be able to move the puck without looking at it. They need to watch out for other players.

13

Some defensive players are very good at blocking shots with their body.

Playing Defense

On defense, players must stop the other team from reaching their goal and scoring points. They can do this by **intercepting** a pass. They can use their strength and speed to check, or bump, an offensive player away from the puck. They can also use their stick or body to block a shot on goal.

Defensive players must be strong to keep the offense from skating by them. They must be quick enough to grab the puck with their sticks when they have a chance.

THE COACH'S CORNER

Each team has two players on defense. However, the offensive players help out on defense when they can. Defensive players help out on offense, too.

Playing Goalie

A goalie stands in front of the team's goal and stops the puck from going into it. This is an important job! A goalie is the last line of defense for the team.

Goalies wear more gear than other players. Their pads are bigger to keep them safe from flying pucks and crashing players. They wear face masks, too. Goalies use a basket-like glove to catch hard shots. The other glove has a wide pad on the back. It's used to block shots.

THE COACH'S CORNER

Long ago, goalies didn't wear masks! In 1959, Canadian Jacques Plante became the first goalie to regularly wear a mask.

A goalie's stick is larger and wider than regular sticks. It's used to block shots.

17

An ice rink has two penalty boxes—one for each team.

The Penalty Box

Hockey has a lot of rules. Players can't pass the puck with their hands. They can't check another player from behind. They can't use their stick to trip or hook other players.

When a player breaks a rule, the referee calls a penalty. The player must sit in an area called the penalty box for at least 2 minutes. Their team must play with one less player during that time! This makes it easier for the other team to score.

THE COACH'S CORNER

The icing rule stops players from shooting the puck all the way down the ice. A team called for icing must have a face-off in their own end.

Making It to the Pros

Playing on a hockey team can be a lot of fun, but there are many other reasons to strap on some skates and hit the rink. Hockey keeps you healthy. It can make you stronger and quicker. It also teaches you the importance of working as a team. No hockey player can win a game alone.

Hockey players who work hard enough often go on to higher levels. Some make it onto professional teams in the National Hockey League (NHL)!

Hockey Gear

stick	• some are wood and some are man-made materials • different lengths depending on player height • long handle • flat, wide blade that makes contact with puck
puck	• hard rubber • 1 inch (2.5 cm) thick • 3 inches (7.6 cm) across
skates	• single sharp blade on each skate • hard outer boot to keep foot and ankle safe
helmet	• hard shell • padded inside • some have a clear plastic shield to keep eyes safe • some have metal cage to keep face safe
pads	• hard shell • padded inside • used to keep many body parts safe, including elbows, knees, legs, shoulders, and chest
gloves	• thick padding • keep hands and fingers safe • goalies have special gloves for catching and blocking shots

Glossary

defending: having to do with guarding something

intercept: to take control of a pass that was meant for a player on the other team

neutral: not belonging to or favoring either side in a contest

penalty: a loss for breaking a rule

professional: earning money from an activity that many people do for fun

referee: an official who makes sure players follow the rules

zone: an area that stands apart from other nearby areas

For More Information

Books

Biskup, Agnieszka. *Hockey: How It Works.* Mankato, MN: Capstone Press, 2010.

Shea, Therese. *Hockey Stars.* New York, NY: Children's Press, 2007.

Thomas, Keltie. *How Hockey Works.* Berkeley, CA: Owlkids Books, 2010.

Websites

Ice Hockey Rules
www.hockey-information.com/ice-hockey-rules.html
Learn more about the basic rules of hockey, as well as penalties, officials, and hockey language.

NHL Kids
www.nhl.com/kids
Catch up on your favorite NHL team and have fun with hockey games and trivia.

Index